The Civilization of the American Indian Series

VICTORIO
and the Mimbres Apaches

NORMAN : UNIVERSITY OF OKLAHOMA PRESS

ORIO

and the Mimbres Apaches

DAN L. THRAPP

By Dan L. Thrapp
(published by the University of Oklahoma Press)

Al Sieber, Chief of Scouts (1964)
The Conquest of Apacheria (1967)
General Crook and the Sierra Madre Adventure (1972)
Victorio and the Mimbres Apaches (1974)

Library of Congress Cataloging in Publication Data

Thrapp, Dan L.
    Victorio and the Mimbres Apaches.

    (The Civilization of the American Indian series, v. 125)
    Bibliography: p.
    1. Victorio, Apache chief, d. 1880. 2. Mimbreño Indians. I. Title.
II. Series.
E99.M63T47   970.3 [B]   72–9269

For Victorio and his fellows ——

They did not understand—who could?—how to live at peace with the aggressive whites, and so in desperation were driven to war, and like the brave men of King's Mountain, the Alamo, Gettysburg, and Pork' Chop Hill, they died, among them some of America's finest sons and daughters.

FOREWORD

Victorio!
America's greatest guerrilla fighter, he was of a motley company: Francis Marion, the swamp fox; William Clarke Quantrill of Lawrence notoriety; John Singleton Mosby, the Confederate ranger; the Burma marauder, Charles Merrill; and a host of others. Victorio was of the fiber of them all, but there was a difference: while they took up arms willingly and fought their vicious skirmishes at what they considered their country's call, Victorio did not.

His long battle was for the preservation of his dying people, because there was no other recourse. In the end, he lost. But not to the Americans, who could never beat him, perhaps because he was one of them, of the essence of their being. No, Victorio never lost to them. He gave up his life, his dreams, his longing to be left alone to live and die in the beloved land of his childhood, youth, and maturity—all of that he lost forever to the rattling muskets of a tightening ring of Mexican soldiers and their auxiliaries on a rugged outcropping in remote Chihuahua, slain when completely helpless, out of ammunition, brought to bay but never truly defeated by those people whom he had fought all of his life and from whom he earned his name: Victorio, the triumphant one.

He did not seek the warpath with the white Americans, this noble and skillful warrior. He was driven to it. Victorio was badgered, "removed," bullied, stolen from, shifted about, lied to and betrayed, separated from his family, starved, threatened, cajoled, made the object of bureaucratic insensitivity at its most obdurate until, frightened by suspicions he found no honest man to quiet, he fled to his mountains and began the dazzling campaign that was to end, a year later, at blood-soaked Tres Castillos.

The story of Victorio is an American saga which has never been told in its entirety, and never will, since too much of the truth died with that Apache and his people. But something of it can be known: the record of his flight, his turning at bay again and again, here, there, in a score of places. This story should be related as much to sting the conscience of the Americans of this day as for the honor and in the memory of a great and valiant one of us.

Almost never did Victorio seek battle with his tormentors. Frequently he grasped for that elusive peace which he must have known was where alone survival lay. But he never shunned a fight, either. No Apache of record, not even the mighty Mangas Coloradas, his predecessor, nor the intractable Cochise, his friend and erstwhile colleague, scored such striking successes against the enemy. His greatness lay partly in that, and even more in how he did it, with what handicaps. Victorio managed all of his movements encumbered with women and children and aged ones, and he kept his people intact through all the battles and withdrawals, the flights and the foraging for supplies; he never abandoned them, and with them finally he was destroyed. In this alone he would be unique.

But there was the added dimension that he waged his war with no more secure system of supply than his wits could contrive. When modern American soldiers campaign, meticulous attention is paid to their needs and desires, their clothing and their food, their weapons, ammunition, support by air, and heavy guns; service battalions follow doggedly in their wake with their mail, their laundry, offering comfort, amusement, caring solicitously for their morale, for otherwise it is feared they will not fight, or at least not well.

Consider, then, Victorio, who had none of these things assured him —not one. It is true that the soldiers he faced, a century ago, were not as pampered as ours today, but the gulf still was vast between what they had and what he had, most notably in arms and ammunition, food and medical supplies, and in discipline, for that too is a soldier's necessity.

Victorio mounted his people on horses and mules they had to steal, fed his followers beef swept off from white ranchers, armed them with weapons and ammunition taken from his victims or swapped for at secret rendezvous with rascally American or Mexican traders eager to exchange the implements of death to hostile Indians in return for marketable livestock from sources unspecified. These unprincipled devotees of *laissez faire* were charged, with some reason, by many an army officer and Indian agent with keeping the war alive, but even if they had not existed Victorio would have found some way to fight on. His people lived on meat and mescal for the most part, and what they looted from occasional wagons seized, the teamsters slain, and mules and oxen added to the fugitive herd. With luck they might find flour in the conveyances, perhaps bright calico for the women, with great good fortune a box or two of rifles or ammunition, though this was rare indeed. Sometimes they found the wagons full of concealed soldiers, an embarrassment quickly forgotten once the sharp skirmish died away.

Unlike Juh, the great Southern Chiricahua war leader, Victorio was not cruel, nor did he torture prisoners, so far as the record shows, although they rarely long enjoyed mortal existence after falling into his hands. But that was the way of the southwestern guerrilla war; adult male prisoners seldom were taken by either side, or retained if somehow captured. Anything went, provided one could seize the advantage. Even such servants of mercy as physicians were not above falling into line. One doctor, called upon to treat an Apache whose leg had been punctured by a bullet, unnecessarily amputated the limb at the hip for no other reason than to make "a ——— good Indian of him," since he believed him to be an inveterate raider.[1] The civil rights activists of recent note would have much work in the Apacheria of the nineteenth century!

Brutality then was a part of life; ruthlessness even more so. Neither was exceptional, nor long remembered. Yet there were whites who shunned them both, and, although this is less well-known, there were Apaches, too, who had no stomach for cruelty or torture and who withdrew when it was practiced, avoiding it when possible.[2] The Apaches, like the whites, were a complex people, with both good and bad among them, and it would be in error to overgeneralize, although, being of a tightly integrated society, they adhered to common customs, as do we all.

Some men rose to greatness among them. Of these the names of a scattering are known to us. Of those remembered, few shine brighter than Victorio, an untutored man driven into hostility by forces he did not fully comprehend, and by a people who made little effort—perhaps were wholly unable—to understand him, or to care for his point of view if they had. This is his story, or as much of it as can now be recovered. It deserves a hearing.

DAN L. THRAPP

Whittier, California

ACKNOWLEDGMENTS

No serious work of history or biography can be done alone, and I am indebted to hundreds of persons who have assisted in one way or another with the preparation of this volume. It would be impossible to list them all, but there are some whose contributions have been outstanding, and I gratefully acknowledge their assistance.

Mrs. Eve Ball, recorder-historian for the Mimbres-Chiricahua Apaches now on the Mescalero Reservation, has been unfailingly helpful with her considerable fund of information. John A. Shapard, married to a great-granddaughter of Loco, and with important connections with the Oklahoma Mimbres, has also been of great assistance. So has Mrs. Clara T. Woody of Miami, Arizona, the ever cooperative historian of central Arizona.

My neighbor, Mrs. Ofelia Davis, born at Chihuahua City, has been graciously helpful in working out sometimes difficult translations from Spanish to English. Of very real help in translation also was Richard Nicholl.

Many friends in Mexico provided indispensable information: Oscar Flores, of Chihuahua, who initially directed me to Tres Castillos and made it possible for me to reach and study the site, supplied me with a copy of Joaquín Terrazas' very rare *Memoirs*, sent me photographs, and generously helped in other ways; Arnaldo Balencia Gallegos, of Galeana, who guided me over the Cerro Mata Ortiz, where that doughty Apache fighter was trapped and slain; Margarita Terrazas Perches and Juan Manuel Terrazas, both of Chihuahua City; the late Ruben Salazar of the *Los Angeles Times* and his secretary, R. A. Bilak, who helped me gain access to the army archives and Joaquín Terrazas' military file at Mexico City.

Jarvis Zeeck of Plainview, Texas, good-naturedly piloted me on aerial reconnaissances over northern Mexico; Alberto Azua, also of Plainview, an Apache descended from the captives of Tres Castillos, supplied information about his people.

Writer C. L. Sonnichsen of Tucson has been characteristically

xiii

generous with information and useful suggestions. Mrs. Buford Richardson, of Socorro, a descendant and biographer of scout Jack Crawford, has been helpful. Tommy Powell, McNary, Texas, conducted me over the site of Fort Quitman, as well as through his reconstruction of it; Mrs. Gladys D. Adamson, Medford, Oregon, and Chester Parker, Globe, Arizona, assisted in my search for H. K. Parker.

Ray Brandes, San Diego, California, was of great bibliographical assistance; Keith Basso, University of Arizona ethnologist, gave important help; Norris F. Schneider, Zanesville, Ohio, supplied information on agent John Greiner, and Richard N. Ellis, of the University of New Mexico, also assisted. Robert Riell of Globe-Phoenix, Arizona, with his accurate recollections of early-day Arizona was of much good-natured help.

No such work as this could get off the ground without the generous, intelligent, and courteous assistance of officials at the National Archives and Records Service, and I would like to mention especially Elmer O. Parker, Old Military Records Division; Miss Jane F. Smith and Richard S. Maxwell, Social and Economics Records Division; and A. P. Muntz, Cartographic and Audiovisual Records Division, who helped in tracking down pertinent maps.

Personnel of many nongovernmental libraries were of immense help. Research on southwestern frontier affairs would be far less successful and pleasant without the cooperation of Mrs. Loretta Davisson of the Arizona Pioneers' Historical Society Library. G. Martin Ruoss of the Zimmerman Library, University of New Mexico, gave me permission to study the Steck Collection and helped in other ways. Mrs. Mary L. Thomas, of the Columbia County Historical Society, New York, assisted in research on John P. Clum and Henry R. Clum, as did Mrs. Virginia F. W. Reichelt, of Tallahassee, Florida. Gerald W. Gillette of the Presbyterian Historical Society of Philadelphia, supplied the copy of a manuscript on Orlanda F. Piper. Superintendent Franklin G. Smith and Robert J. Holden, of the Fort Davis National Historic Site, were helpful with photographs and in other ways. *Los Angeles Times'* artist James Francavilla was generous with his talents.

Certain field trips were made more pleasant and productive in the enjoyable company of Bud Shapard, James A. Walker, Wendel Towse, and Philip Van Strander, and I am grateful to them all.

DAN L. THRAPP

CONTENTS

ILLUSTRATIONS

All photographs not otherwise credited were made by the author.

MAPS

VICTORIO
and the Mimbres Apaches

I

The Making of a Warrior

The Apaches were a numerous, warlike people, moving into the Southwest when they first appear in written history. It is said they did not enter Arizona until after the middle of the sixteenth century,[1] although this is disputed. When the first explorers and beaver trappers from the United States penetrated the region, early in the nineteenth century, Apache bands were settled semipermanently in the area that concerns us, southern New Mexico and eastern Arizona.

At this period the Apaches may be divided into two great divisions: the eastern, including the Jicarillas, Lipans, and Kiowa-Apaches, all culturally akin to the Southern Plains Indians; and the western division. This included four principal groups: the Navahos, the Mescaleros, the so-called Western Apaches, and the Chiricahuas. The last, our primary interest, were split into three bands: the central group, which inhabited the Chiricahua and Dragoon mountains of Arizona, and whose most famous leader was Cochise; the southern band, often called the Southern Apaches, or Pinery Apaches, based partly in the Sierra Madre of Mexico, and with whom Geronimo and Juh were associated; and the Eastern Chiricahuas. These last inhabited the country from the Río Grande to the present Arizona line, and from the Mexican border northward to beyond the Datil Range in New Mexico.[2] Their greatest leader in early southwestern history was Mangas Coloradas, but after his murder by California soldiers they developed others to succeed him.

East of the Eastern Chiricahuas, beyond the Río Grande, lived the Mescaleros, with whom they sometimes associated, although a bit stiffly.

The Eastern Chiricahuas themselves included two major groupings: one called the Mogollon or Mogollones Apaches, normally dwelling about the mountains of that name but who had a close relationship with the eastern bands of the Western Apaches; and the remainder, our primary concern. These were known by many names: Coppermine Apaches, Mimbres or Mimbreños, Gila Apaches, Warm

3

Springs, or Ojo Caliente, Apaches, and others. Originally these names may have had valid geographical meaning, but in the jostling about that followed the influx of white settlers such titles became rootless. Thus a name might refer to some small party that happened to camp near the copper mines, or along the Mimbres or Gila rivers, or in the vicinity of Warm Springs or Ojo Caliente, rather than to any generic grouping. But in the beginning, when the names of the bands bore significance, it is the Mimbres Apaches that are of interest, for Victorio was of that people. It was estimated that he was approximately fifty-five years of age at his death in 1880, which suggests he was born about 1825, give or take a few years. It was about the time the Santa Fe Trail was opened, bringing the first Anglo traders and rovers to this northern frontier of Spanish America.

No account of Victorio can ignore the enigma of his birth.

To most Anglos he was simply an Apache, albeit a great one. To Spanish-Americans, however, he had been born a Mexican, was captured as a boy, raised among the Indians, but always with a Mexican birthright—a belief that was based, to some extent, upon a general impression south of the border that he was "too intelligent" for an Indian.[3] What is the truth?

Unfortunately, at this date, one cannot state definitely that he was one or the other, for none of his contemporaries discussed it or, for that matter, appear to have heard the question. Would the speculation then that he was Mexican perhaps be of recent origin? This suspicion is supported by a general lack of early references in Anglo literature to his having been anything but an Apache. If the contrary is true, Americans of his times appear never to have heard of it, no matter how strongly the legend persists in Chihuahua.[4]

A niece of the then-owner of the ranch on which Tres Castillos is situated asserted in 1948 that Victorio had been stolen as a boy from Hacienda del Carmen, owned by the family of Luis Terrazas, later a fabulously wealthy stockman and governor of Chihuahua, of whom we shall hear more. She wrote that nothing was heard of the child until "many years later, when a very old-looking man . . . Rufino Padilla, who had been an Indian captive for four years . . . reported that during his own captivity he had seen a young and daring Indian lad whose resemblance to the father of the missing boy could not be mistaken or overlooked."[5]

If "Rufino Padilla" was the captive Felipe Padilla freed after the Apache disaster at Tres Castillos, which is a possibility, he was then ten years old and, if he had been held four years, was six when captured.[6] In that case, by reason of his youth, his reported impression of Victorio's resemblance to the Mexican who had lost a son many years earlier should not receive undue weight, although it must not be arbitrarily dismissed, either. Assuredly El Carmen saw many Indian raids and occasionally lost children to the hostiles.

Archtypical of the great self-sufficient haciendas of northern Mexico a century and one-half ago,[7] there remain even today grim portions of the chocolate-colored twenty-foot walls that once enclosed the El Carmen headquarters, standing as mute evidence of defense against the swirling bands of implacable Apaches and Comanches alternately sweeping its environs. Touches of the vast wealth El Carmen represented remain, too, in the ornately cobbled roadway through the thick walls, the worn but elaborate gates, the extensive settlement enclosed, all attesting to the resolution and the grim pride of the hacendados who held this land to ultimate triumph over the savage hordes.

Some of the children rudely snatched from this fortress-ranch did indeed rise to prominence among the wild peoples of the north. Costales, for example, taken as a child from El Carmen, became a subchief of the Mimbres Apaches before he was murdered by Mexicans, his fellow nationals, perhaps even his blood relatives.[8]

The legend of the Mexican origin of Victorio appears in many variations. At least one authority who appears to believe that Victorio, like Costales, was Mexican thinks both were seized in Sonora to the west, while a Chihuahua historical journal, reporting the early kidnaping of Victorio, added the detail that he was a mestizo.[9] However, the validity of the El Carmen theory runs against this objection: the difficulty, not to say the impossibility, of tracing a given captive from childhood through the vicissitudes of a wild and seminomadic youth, and his development into a warrior and eventually a chief. The implausibility of this being accomplished successfully is enhanced by the fact that the Apaches took numerous captives. Some of their raiding was largely for that purpose; the strength of the tribe was to a great extent maintained by the constant influx of new blood, from boy, girl, and women captives.[10]

There is, it should be mentioned in passing, yet another theory of his Mexican ancestry. This states that he was one Francisco Cedillos, Jr., who was given the name of Victoria, his aunt, whom he pleaded with his Apache captors to be allowed to rejoin. They, understanding

5

but little Spanish, caught only the word "Victoria," which they applied to him. This ingenious version has him born in the community of Vado de Cedillos, said to be forty miles down the Río Grande from Juarez.[11] However engaging this yarn, it runs into difficulty with the substantial evidence that Victorio was not so named until he already was a war leader and had earned the title.

The legend that he was of Mexican birth might be supposed strengthened by the fact that he bore a Spanish name, but this was not uncommon among the Chiricahuas. In 1877 a census was taken of the Ojo Caliente Apaches, Victorio's band. Heads of families numbered 177, and of these 84, or almost half, bore names clearly of Spanish derivation, while an additional 22 had Anglo cognomens, at least for the purpose of the count.[12] Thus the fact that Victorio bore a name of Spanish origin says nothing of his own.

Obviously, even if he was known by a Spanish name in what might be termed his "public" life, he must also have had an Indian name by which he was known to his people. Goodwin says that his Apache name was Bidu-ya, which he believed a corruption of "Victorio."[13] Jason Betzinez, an Apache who accompanied Victorio on certain occasions and later campaigned with Geronimo, believed Victorio's name was Beduiat, which closely approximates Goodwin. But Betzinez adds that "it may be that the Mexicans made Victorio out of that," which would reverse the theory advanced by the ethnologist.[14] Goodwin believed that when an Indian name truly was a corruption of a Spanish name, it usually belonged to "captives taken in Sonora and raised among the Apache,"[15] but he did not aver that Victorio was such a case.

There is very good evidence, on the other hand, that he was not Mexican. Gillett M. Griswold, who has compiled the most authoritative and exhaustive genealogy of the Warm Springs-Chiricahua Apaches ever assembled, writes of Victorio that he was born about 1820 in New Mexico, and adds: "He was a member of the Chihennes band," with no reference whatever to his having been Mexican or even part-Mexican.[16]

The Prescott *Arizonian*, shortly after his final bust-out in 1879, said:

VICTORIO THE INDIAN CHIEF.—Having been asked about Victorio the Apache war chief we publish the following description:
Victorio claims to be the hereditary chief of the Apaches, directly descended on his father's side from a long line of royal ancestors. In this he

is distinguished from the other chiefs in the same band, Loco and Nana, who have achieved their own greatness. Victorio was born great. He is almost 50 years old, 5 feet 9½ inches in height, with irregular but not unpleasant features, s[t]olid countenance, his long hair plentifully sprinkled with grey, hanging over his shoulders.[17]

Newspaper articles are not infallible, but the Prescott *Arizonian*, during its brief existence of less than a year, was edited by John Marion, an unusually able and reliable newsman, one of the true pioneers of central Arizona, and one unlikely to be guilty of gross inaccuracy.[18] Betzinez, the literate and honest Apache, in his memoirs has Victorio protesting a removal to San Carlos from Ojo Caliente with the expression, "This country belongs to my people as it did to my forefathers,"[19] scarcely the words of a onetime captive and by blood a Mexican rather than an Apache.

Victorio became a head chief, though that in itself does not prove he was born an Indian.[20] A Chiricahua informant told the reliable ethnologist Morris E. Opler that "a prisoner who has grown up with the Chiricahua and has accepted the life might even become a war leader if he is brave and successful enough."[21] This does not imply that a captive could ever become a head chief, however, and although Opler mentions Victorio several times in various contexts, he never suggests that he was anything but a Chiricahua by birth.

I have read the surviving letters and reports of every Eastern Chiricahua agent from 1849, when most of the Apache lands came under control of the United States, until well after Victorio's death, and no one of them ever suggested that this leader was anything but an Apache, while warriors of other than Apache descent are invariably identified as such. Nor did any of the numerous army officers who operated against or were otherwise associated with the Apaches. If it was believed while he was alive that Victorio was by birth anything but an Indian, it was a well-kept secret; no whisper of it has survived.

Nor do descendants of his people today believe that he was anything but an Apache. Mrs. Eve Ball, who has interviewed about sixty Mescaleros and descendants of Victorio's band, including James Kaywaykla, who as a boy was at the battle of Tres Castillos, said that her informants unanimously believed him to have been wholly Indian. "James Kaywaykla replied when I questioned him about this, 'If he were not, Nana would have told me.' So, he added, would many others," she said.[22] Moses and Raymond Loco, grandsons of Chief

7

Loco, Victorio's closest colleague, said that Victorio was not a Mexican, adding, "none of the Apache stories about him have him as anything but an Apache," and, had he been Mexican, that fact "would have been a key part of each story told about him."[23]

It is perhaps coincidental that the only known photograph of Victorio has been considerably toned down in an artist's reproduction, so that a face that seems patently Apache in the photograph appears possibly Mexican in the portrait painted from it. The somewhat wild appearance of Victorio in this famous portrait is due, I have been told, to his head band having fallen off in a vigorous struggle which accompanied his being held for the camera by two men who do not show in the picture.

As an illustration of the fact that an individual, once a captive, ever was known as such, Costales, seized from El Carmen and later becoming a subchief of the Mimbres, was always identified as such by Indians and whites alike.[24] There never appears any such acknowledgment that Victorio was Mexican or had significant Spanish blood.

It would be unfair to leave the subject without giving the reader an inkling as to where the author stands. Borrowing from the recently devised technique of weather forecasters, assessing an uncertain matter in terms of percentages, I would suppose that the chances are about 85 to 15; that is, 85 per cent that Victorio was born an Apache, and 15 per cent that he was not. C. L. Sonnichsen, who advances the Mexican birth theory without taking sides, concedes that, in any event, he would have been a child when seized, was raised as an Indian, and "passed for a Mimbres or Gila Apache of the Warm Springs band. Their people were his people, their gods were his gods."[25]

An Apache was born into a ritualistic and complex culture geared toward preparing him for war and raiding, if a boy, or for being the wife and mother of warriors, if a girl. Yet, even during the period of most activity, from eighteen to forty-five, the man spent less than one-third of his time—usually far less—at actively hostile pursuits. Afterward, if wise and experienced, and if he survived, he became a much listened-to elder from forty-five to sixty. His influence then gradually waned with his strength and his memories, until he passed into death at some indeterminate old age.[26]

The baby's first home, one for many months and which bred into him a sense of security he never was to lose, was the artful cradleboard, still used by wise Apache parents. The infant was laced in at